WHAT T
BIBLE SAYS®

The Great
White
Throne
Judgment

What the Bible Says:

The Great White Throne Judgment

Published by: Armor Books
P. O. Box 1050
Lawrenceville, GA 30045
Web Site: http://www.armorbooks.com
All rights reserved.

This book and parts thereof may not be reproduced in any form, stored in a retrieval system or transmitted in any form by any means—electronic, mechanical, photocopy, recording or otherwise—without prior written permission of the publisher, except as provided by United States of America copyright law.

This is a derivative writing taken from the collective works of the late Finis Jennings Dake, and used by permission of the copyright holders. Unless otherwise noted, all Scripture quotations are from the Holy Bible, King James Version

Copyright © 2003 by Armor Books

First Printing 2003

Printed in the United States of America.

ISBN: 1-55829-083-4 (paperback)

01 02 03 04 05   87654321

CONTENTS

PREFACE

For many Christians, the Bible is a book of mystery, full of hidden meaning only to be understood by pastors and seminarians who have devoted lifetimes to uncovering the truths found within its pages. Latin was the language of the Bible for centuries, and many still approach the Scriptures as if they were written in a foreign tongue. A few stories are learned in Sunday School, a handful of popular verses memorized, but many Christians fear to turn the pages of their Bibles into unfamiliar territory.

But there is no reason to be afraid. The Bible is the easiest book in the world to understand. You don't need to be a pastor or have a seminary degree. God designed the Bible to be understood by everyone, and the truths He intended for us to learn are easily found within its pages.

The "*What the Bible Says*" booklets are designed to illustrate simple biblical truths

4

on topics that many consider to be particularly difficult to grasp. This book strives to let the Bible speak for itself, and therefore, a comprehensive list of Scripture references for each of the topics discussed will be presented. Although it's not necessary to look up each and every reference in order to understand what the Bible is saying on a particular topic, we'll focus on the primary references, and give you a thorough list of supporting scriptures for you to study on your own.

HOW TO UNDERSTAND THE BIBLE

Here's the most important rule to follow when studying the Bible: You must take the Bible literally wherever it is at all possible. Obviously, there are times when the language of the Bible cannot be taken literally, it is then we know it is to be understood figuratively. When this is the case, it is our job to find the literal truth conveyed by the figurative language, just as if it were expressed in literal language without the use of figures. For more on this topic, see Chapter 2, "Biblical Studies."

FIGURATIVE LANGUAGE OF THE BIBLE

The Bible contains some figurative language. A lot of confusion is caused when literal passages of Scripture are mistakenly understood figuratively, and the same holds true for Scripture that is interpreted as literal, when it is obviously figurative in nature. So what is figurative language in the Bible? How can we recognize it when we find it? Simply put, figurative language, or a "figure of speech" occurs when we use words in a different sense from that which is ordinarily given them. Figures of speech are used to give emphasis and to add attraction and variety to human expression. It is important to note that they are never used for the purpose of doing away with literal truth. Instead, figures of speech set forth literal truth in another form than that in which it could be literally expressed. What we're looking for is the literal truth found in the figurative language. Above all, we must not permit figures of speech to do away with the intended truth. If we fail to understand the literal truth expressed by the figure of speech, then it has failed in its purpose.

Now that we understand figures of speech, how can we tell whether a particular statement is intended to be understood literally or figuratively? It's easy! There's a fundamental rule to keep in mind when determining whether the language is literal or figurative: Every statement in the Bible is to be understood literally, when at all possible, and where it is clear that it is literal; otherwise, it is figurative. In other words, what cannot be literal must be figurative. The subject matter itself will always make this clear.

> *Above all, we must not permit figures of speech to do away with the intended truth. If we fail to understand the literal truth expressed by the figure of speech, then it has failed in its purpose.*

There are two kinds of figures of speech we find in the Bible: first, there are those involving only a word, as in Gal. 2:9 where Peter, James, and John are called "pillars" of the church; second, there are those involving a thought expressed in several words or sentences, such as the parable, allegory, symbol, type, riddle, fable, and enigma.

GOD'S PROMISES ARE ESPECIALLY SIMPLE

We've stated that many people think the Bible is hard to understand. In particular, this belief is held by many concerning the prophecies, the proverbs, and some figures of speech. However, these seemingly difficult parts of the Bible are no more difficult to understand than the sections of the Bible that deal with history, or those that many consider to be "simple." Prophecy is nothing more than history written beforehand and should be understood in this light. All riddles, allegories, types, symbols, and figures of speech are either explained in Scripture, or are clear in themselves as to their true meaning.

When it comes to the promises of God, there shouldn't be any misunderstanding about what they say or mean. Every promise of God is a simple statement of obligation to men that God will give them certain benefits when they meet certain conditions. All the promises of God are conditional, as can be seen in the Scriptures themselves. If you want to receive the promised benefits, you must accept the promise for what it says and meet the conditions required. You can then depend upon the fulfillment of God's promise *in this life*. Since God cannot lie, man is assured that what God has promised He is abundantly able to perform. None of God's promises need further interpretation. All that we must do is act upon what the Bible says and believe that God's promise will be fulfilled in our lives. Do not attach any other conditions to God's promises than what is plainly written. When the conditions are met the blessings will be realized. As the Apostle Paul writes in 2 Cor. 1:20, "For ALL the promises of God in Him are yea, and in Him Amen, unto the glory of God by us."

Chapter One

THE GREAT WHITE THRONE JUDGEMENT

THE SEVEN JUDGMENTS OF SCRIPTURE

It is a commonly–held belief among Christians that history will culminate with a final judgment, during which all people will stand before their Creator. Those who, in the words of the Apostle Paul, have "fought a good fight" and have finished the course set before them, will recieve their reward. But for those who have rejected God, eternal punishment awaits.

That these events will take place, there is no doubt—the Bible is very clear that judgment will come, both for the righteous and the unrighteous. However, the Scriptures do not speak of a single event during which the righteous and the wicked will be judged. Instead, there will be angels and different classes of men to be judged, and each class will be judged separately and at different times. There are   seven judgment events for both angels and men—some have taken place already and other are yet to occur. In the following pages we'll take a look at each of these judgments. We'll begin by looking at the greatest judgment of them all—the Great White Throne Judgment.

I. The Great White Throne Judgment (Rev. 20:11-15)

> And I saw a great white throne, and him that sat on it, from whose face the earth and the heaven fled away; and there was found no place for them. And I saw the dead, small and great, stand before God; and the books were opened: and another book was opened, which is the book of life: and the dead were judged out of those things which were written in the books, according to their works. And the sea gave up the dead which were in it;

and death and hell delivered up the dead which were in them: and they were judged every man according to their works. And death and hell were cast into the lake of fire. This is the second death. And whosoever was not found written in the book of life was cast into the lake of fire (Rev. 20:11-15)

This passage will be fulfilled after the Millennium and the revolt of Satan, for it was immediately after these events (referred to in Rev. 20:1-10) that John saw a great white throne occupied by God, from whose face the earth and Heaven fled away. This is no doubt the same throne seen throughout the book of Revelation. However, this passage is the only place that a description of the throne is given. God, the occupant of the throne, is described in the preceeding verses, but the throne itself is not (Rev. 4:2-3, 9-11; 5:1-14; 6:16; 7:7-9; 14:1-5; 19:4; 21:5; 22:1-5).

This portion of Scripture speaks of real people, places and events. This passage mentions that the "earth and heaven fled away." The Greek word for "face" is *prosopon*, meaning the "countenance," "aspect," "appearance," "surface," "front view," "outward appearance," "face," and "person." It is used nine times in Revelation and is the only word translated as "face," in both the singular and plural. It is used here, not as an anthropomorphism (a figure of speach in which human attributes are given to someone or something that doesn't really possess them), but as an affirmation of the reality of God, and the assurance that judgment will surely come. God is not some impersonal, mystical force, but has a spiritual body and an outward appearance, and is "real" in every sense of the word. We see the word "face" used in the same way in the

The word "face" is used here, not as an anthropomorphism, but as an affirmation of the reality of God, and the assurance that judgment will surely come. God is not some impersonal, mystical force, but has a spiritual body and an outward appearance, and is "real" in every sense of the word.

following passages: (Rev. 4:7; 6:16; 7:11; 9:7; 10:1; 11:16; 12:14; 22:4). This is further proven by its usage in the rest of the New Testament where it appears forty-eight times, and always refers to bodily presence, actual faces, or external appearance.

Revelation 20:11-15 refers to God and His throne. The fact that Christ and His throne are not mentioned here does not necessarily imply that they will be absent. Both Christ and the Father will be present and have a part in the final judgment.

Now it's time to take a closer look at the Great White Throne Judgment. In all its varied aspects, this judgment may be understood from the following facts in Scripture:

The Judges

There will be more than one judge at the Great White Throne Judgment. We find, in a survey of the New Testament, that there will be at least three judges involved in this event:

1. God the Father is spoken of as the judge of all men (Heb. 12:23-24; 13:4; Rev. 6:10; Acts 17:30, 31; Rom. 2:12-16).
2. God the Son is also spoken of as the judge of the world (Jn. 5:19-27; Acts 10:42; 17:30, 31; 2 Tim. 4:8; Rev.19:11).
3. Both the Father and the Son will be judges (Acts 17:31; Rom. 2:16).
4. God the Father will judge by His Son (Acts 17:31; Rom. 2:16).
5. God the Father will decree; the Son will execute (Jn. 5:22-27; Rom.1:32; 2:5).
6. The saints will have part in this judgment (1 Cor. 6:2-3; Rev. 3:21).

The Subjects Judged

We mentioned earlier that the Great White Throne Judgment will not be a general judgment of angels and men. However, there will be two distinct groups that will face judgment during this time:

(1) Wicked men of the whole human

race, except the Beast, False Prophet, the goat nations, tares, etc., will be the subjects of God's judgment (Acts 17:31; Rom.3:6; Rev. 20:11-15). That those who appear at the judgment of the nations will not also be judged at the final judgment seems clear from many verses, including Mt. 13:30, 39-43, 49, 50; 24:51; 25:30, 41,

> *Those judged at this time will be the wicked dead of all ages, whereas those judged at the judgment of the nations will be the nations living on earth when Christ returns to set up His eternal kingdom.*

46; Rev. 14:9-11; 19:20, 21; 20:10. These already will have had sentence pronounced upon them a thousand years before the final judgment, so it would not be necessary to judge them again. Those judged at this time will be the wicked dead of all ages, whereas those who stand before God at the judgment of the nations will be the nations living on earth when Christ returns to set up His eternal kingdom.

(2)   Both Peter and Jude refer to the angels "that sinned" and "are now bound" in Tartarus.

They will also be loosed from their long confinement in chains and be judged during this time of judgment (2 Pet. 2:4; Jude 6, 7).

The Time of the Judgment

This judgment will take place after the Millennium and after the doom of Satan in the Lake of Fire is realized (Rev. 20:7-15). It is called "the day of judgment" and so there must be a definite time set for it (Mt. 10:15; 11:24; 12:36; Acts 17:31; 2 Pet. 2:4; Jude 6, 7). The purpose of the Millenium (the 1,000-year reign of Christ) is to suppress all rebellion (1 Cor. 15:24-28) and the final defeat of Satan and his hosts at the end of the Millennium must be accomplished before this judgment occurs.

The Place of the Judgment

The judgment is to take place before the Great White Throne of God, which will still be in Heaven, for it is not to come down to the earth until after the renovation of the earth by fire and after the New Heaven and the New Earth are completed (Rev. 21:1-5). The

17

Apostle Peter adds support for this arguement in 2 Pet. 3:7 where he states that the renovation of the earth will take place during the final judgment. We see the throne mentioned again in Rev. 20:11, which describes the events surrounding the final judgment.

The Purpose of the Judgment

The Great White Throne Judgment is convened for a specific purpose. Men are given a fair trial, but it is not only their actions that will be judged during this time. Motivations and secret thoughts are impossible to judge by earthly standards, but God, who is able to see our thoughts as clearly as our deeds, will be the judge. The purpose of the Great White Throne Judgment will be:

1. To give every man a fair trial before condemnation and punishment (Acts 17:31).
2. To judge the "secrets of men" (Rom. 2:16).
3. To judge all idle words (Mt. 12:36).
4. To judge all the works, thoughts, actions and sins of man (1 Tim. 5:24; 1 Pet. 1: 17; Rev. 20:12-13; 22:12; Rom. 2:5-6).

The Basis of Judgment

Paul tells the Romans that those who reject God are "without excuse," for

> The invisible things of him from the creation of the world are clearly seen, being understood by the things that are made (Rom. 1:20)

Those facing this judgment will be judged according to this law, as well as others:

1. The law of conscience (Rom. 2:12-16; Heb. 10:27).
2. The law of memory (Lk. 16:25).
3. The law of Moses (Rom. 2:12-16; Rev. 20:11-15).
4. The law of character (Heb. 3:8-10, 15; Eph. 4:19).
5. The gospel (Rom. 2:12-16; Jn. 12:47, 48; Rev. 20:11-15).
6. All acts and words (Mt. 12:36; Lk. 12: 2-9; Jn. 3:18).
7. The Book of Life (Rev. 20:11-15).

A man who passes through this judgment will have no excuse or criticism of the sentence passed, regardless of what the decision will be, for in a sense he will be his own judge. The actual manifestation of his failure to live up to his conscience, the law, or the gospel, the fact that his sins and misdeeds are like mountains before him—in his conscience and in his character—and the absence of his name in the Book of Life, will automatically condemn him.

The "books" mentioned in Rev. 20:12 do not refer to the records of men written in books and kept by a recording angel, for we have no knowledge of such in Scripture, but they contain the Word of God, which is to judge man in the day of judgment, as seen above. The Book of Life is mentioned in Ex. 32:32-33; Ps. 69:25-29; Dan. 12:1; Lk. 10:20; Phil. 4:3; Rev. 3:5; 13:8; 17:8; 20:12, 15; 21:27; 22:19, and has reference to the book in which the name of every man who is to enter into eternal life is recorded. This book alone will be sufficient to condemn a man.

It is not clear from Rev. 20:11-15 what will be the basis of judgment for the angels in Tartarus, but they probably know upon what basis their judgment is to be as well as does man. It seems clear that only "the dead are judged out of those things which are written in the books," and that they are judged "according to their works." It is also clear that it will be an individual judgment, for it is recorded that "every man" will be judged according to his works.

The dead who are dealt with here could not include the angels, for the former are the occupants of "death and hell." This proves that Hades, the present and temporary Hell, is different from the Lake of Fire or eternal Hell. The sinner is placed in Hades to await his committal to the Lake of Fire, even as the criminal is placed in a jail before he is tried and sentenced to the penitentiary. The sinner is guilty while in Hades,

> *The sinner is placed in Hades to await his committal to the Lake of Fire, even as the criminal is placed in a jail before he is tried and sentenced to the penitentiary. The sinner is guilty while in Hades, although he is not formally condemned before the final judgment. Therefore, he suffers fire in Hades as well as in the Lake of Fire.*

although he is not formally condemned before the final judgment. Therefore, he suffers fire in Hades as well as in the Lake of Fire (Lk. 16:19-31), just like a man suffers confinement in jail before he goes to the penitentiary.

The Result of the Judgment

(1)   If anyone's name is not found to be written in the Book of Life, he will be cast into the Lake of Fire. Hades is the present abiding place for the souls of the wicked dead. The word "Hades" never refers to the literal grave where bodies are placed after death. Rather, it is a place of consciousness, where men are in torment until the resurrection. Those whose names are not written in the Book of Life—all human beings in Hades and "in death," along with the angels in Tartarus, the demons in the Abyss and every other rebel against God—will be cast into the Lake of Fire to be punished forever (Rev. 2: 11; 14:9-11; 20:10-15; 21:8; Mk. 9:42-48; Mt. 18:9; 24:51; 25:41, 46; Isa. 66:22-24).

Eight Facts About Tartarus:

1. A prison for angels (2 Pet. 2:4)
2. Located under the earth (2 Pet. 2:4)
3. A place of confinement for angels until the judgment (2 Pet. 2:4; Rev. 20:11-15; Jude 6)
4. A place visited by Christ when He went to Hell (Ps. 16:10; 1 Pet. 3:19)
5. A place of darkness (Jude 6-7)
6. A place of eternal fire (Jude 7)
7. A place of vengeance (Jude 7)
8. The word is used only here, but in Greek writings, *tartarus* was held to be a place in the earth lower than Hades where the Titans, the primeval deities or the giants who were supposed to be the first children of the earth and even older than the Greek gods, were cast when they lost their war with Zeus.

(2) Varying degrees of punishment will be the result of this judgment, just as various degrees of reward will be the result of the judgment of the saints at the Judgment Seat of Christ (Mt. 7:2; 10:15; 11:22-24; 12:41-45; 23:12-14; Mk. 6:11; Lk. 10:14; 11:31, 32; Rev. 20:11-15). Hell, as far as the torment of fire is concerned, will be alike for all the lost, as much as Heaven, as far as bliss and comfort are concerned, will be alike for all the redeemed. The degrees of punishment will come through the torment of the conscience and the inward self over the deeds committed, which will eat more deeply into the inner-most being as the ages come and go into the eternal future. In contrast to the wicked and their punishment, the rewards for the saints will be ever–increasing glory and splendor as the ages come and go into all eternity.

> *The judgment passed upon each individual will be eternal. The same terms that are used in describing the eternity of God are used in describing the eternity of Hell, so if one is eternal, the other one must be also.*

24

The Length of the Judgment

The judgment passed upon each individual will be eternal. The same terms that are used in describing the eternity of God are used in describing the eternity of Hell, so if one is eternal, the other one must be also (Isa. 66:22-24; Mt. 5:22, 29, 30; 10:28; 13:42, 50; 18:9; 23:15, 33; 24:51; 25:30, 41-46; Mk. 9:42-48; Lk. 12:5; Heb. 6:2; 10:26-31; Rev. 14:9-11; 19:20; 20:10-15; 21:8).

> *First, if physical death would have been the only penalty, then the penalty for sin would be paid at death and all who die physically would be free from sin and would go immediately to Heaven, because the penalty would be paid and they would not be guilty any longer.*

It is important to be aware that there is a reason why man's punishment is eternal. First, if physical death would have been the only penalty, then the penalty for sin would be paid at death and all who die physically would be free from sin and would go immediately to Heaven, because the penalty would be paid and they would not be guilty any longer. This would not be a penalty, but a reward. If this were true, then there could be no such thing as redemption, for all die physically.

Second, The penalty could not be spiritual death alone, because spiritual death is the state of sin into which *all* sinners go when they become sinful. This state of sin is spoken of as being "dead in trespasses and sins" (Eph. 2:1-9; Col. 2:13).

Even with civil governments, the crime committed does not correspond to the duration of the penalty. The length of time spent breaking the law has nothing to do with the length of time one must suffer the guilt and punishment.

The penalty, therefore, must be eternal (or endless) death or separation from God. Death is separation from the purpose for which a person was made. Physical death is the separation of the inner man from the outer man (Jas. 2: 26), and spiritual death is the separation of the soul from God by sin (Isa. 59:2). Therefore, if either one of these deaths were the penalty for the sin, the penalty would be paid once

26

spiritual and physical death was experienced, and God could not hold men guilty any longer, because the penalty would have been paid.

In spite of the reasons listed above, some still object to the idea of endless separation from God and the corresponding eternal torment on the grounds that it is out of proportion with the time spent committing sin in this life. If this is a difficult

> *It is the design or intent of the sin committed that constitutes the moral aspect of the action and not the length of time taken to commit it. It is not the number of sins and the time used in committing them, but the guilt of the sin that deserves endless punishment.*

concept to grasp, remember that even with civil governments, the crime committed does not correspond to the duration of the penalty. The length of time spent breaking the law has nothing to do with the length of time one must suffer the guilt and punishment.

It is the design or intent of the sin committed that constitutes the moral aspect of the action and not the length of time taken to commit it. It is not the number of sins and the time used in committing them, but the guilt of the sin that deserves endless punishment.

II. The Judgment of the Believer's Sin (Jn. 12:31-32)

1. *Subject*: The believer as to sin (Rom. 6: 10; Heb. 9:25-28).
2. *Time*: On the cross (Jn. 3:14; 1 Pet. 2: 24; Jn. 17:4).
3. *Place*: Calvary (Lk. 23:33; Jn. 19:17-24).
4. *Basis*: Christ's perfect work (Jn. 3:16; 5:24; Rom. 6:8).
5. *Result*: Death to Christ, justification to believers (Rom. 4:1-25; 5:l-ll, 15-21; 8:1-16). This judgment deals with the believer as a sinner.

III. The Believer's Judgment of Himself (1 Cor. 11:31, 32)

1. *Subjects*: Believers walking in the light (1 Jn. 1:7).
2. *Time*: During this life (Eph. 4:22-32; Col. 3:5-17).

3. *Place*: In his own life (Rom. 8:1-16; Heb. 12:5-11).
4. *Basis*: Obedience to God and His Word (Jas. 1:22-25).
5. *Result*: Chastisement or approval from God (Heb. 12:5-11). This judgment deals with the believer as a son during his earthly pilgrimage.

IV. The Judgment of the Believer's Works (Rom. 14:10; 2 Cor. 5:10)

1. *Subjects*: Believers (Gal. 6:8; Eph. 6:8; Col. 3:24; Rom. 14; 2 Cor. 5:10).
2. *Time*: Between the rapture and the Second Coming (Lk. 14:14).
3. *Place*: In Heaven (1 Cor. 9:24-27; Rom. 14:10; 2 Cor. 5:10).
4. *Basis*: Works, both good and bad (1 Cor. 3:11-15; 2 Cor. 5:10; Rom. 14; Col. 3; Mt. 16:27; Rom. 2:6; 2 Tim. 4: 14; Rev. 2:23; 22:12). Believers will be judged concerning:

    (a) Doctrines (Rom. 2:14-16; 14).

    (b) Conduct to others (Mt. 18; Rom. 14).

(c) Carnal traits (Col. 3; Rom. 1–2; 8: 1-13; 14:1-23).

(d) Words (Mt. 12:32-37; Rom. 14).

(e) Things that affect others: slander, quarrels, idle words, foolishness, joking, debts, broken promises, wrong dealings, etc. (Rom. 1:29-32; 1 Cor. 6:9-11; Gal. 5:19-21; Col. 3; Eph. 4: 1-32; 5:1-33; Rom. 12:1-21; 14:1-23).

(f) Things that affect themselves: neglected opportunities, wasted talents, loose living, lack of spirituality, etc. (Rom. 2:14-16; Heb. 2:1-4; Gal. 5:1-26; 6:1-10; Col. 3).

(g) Things that affect God: refusal to walk in the light, disobedience, rejection, failure to cooperate and yield to the Spirit, etc. (1 Cor. 12; Rom. 12; Eph. 4: 1-32; 5:1-33).

5. *Result*: Reward or loss of reward, but never the loss of the soul for those wrong doings, providing they have been forgiven (1 Cor. 3:11-15). This judgment deals with the believer as a servant (Rom. 14; 2 Cor. 5:10-11; 1 Cor. 3:11-15).

6. *Illustration*: Analysis of the zeal of a candidate for a crown in glory.

The following analysis was taken from the experience of a prominent Christian worker who enjoyed a great deal of success in his ministry. His church was crowded, souls were being saved and everything seemed to be going well. One day he went home after a successful Sunday at church and fell asleep in a parlor chair. An angel appeared to him and asked him, "How is your zeal?" He was proud of his zeal and answered, "Fine!" The angel then asked him for his zeal and he pulled it out of his bosom and gave it to him. The angel put it in a crucible and put a fire under it until it melted. He then poured it out on the hearth and it formed strata. He then broke it in pieces and put each piece on scales and weighed it and gave the following analysis to the minister:

> *"How is your zeal?" He was proud of his zeal and answered, "Fine!" The angel then asked him for his zeal and he pulled it out of his bosom and gave it to him.*

TOTAL WEIGHT 100 POUNDS

Of this analysis there proves to be:

1. Bigotry...............................11 parts
2. Personal ambition................22 parts
3. Love of praise.....................19 parts
4. Pride of denomination..........15 parts
5. Love of authority.................12 parts
6. Pride of talents ....14 parts
7. Love of God ....4 parts
8. Love of man ....3 parts

This Christian worker said his anger arose and he began to deny the truth of this analysis, but the angel walked toward the door, stopped and looked back with pity in his eyes and said, "May God save you," and walked out the door. The minister woke with conviction seizing his heart; falling to the floor he prayed to be saved—not from the fires of Hell—but from himself. He prayed until the refining fire of the Spirit purged him of self and thereafter he was more successful than ever. This refining process is no doubt the greatest need of the modern church (Rom. 6; 12; Gal. 5; Col. 3; Eph. 4 and 5).

V. The Judgment of Israel
(Ezek. 20:33-44)

Ezekiel prophesies of a time in which God will bring judgment to those of Israel who have rebelled. That this prophecy has not yet been fulfilled is clear—Israel does not yet know the Lord:

> And I will bring you out from the people, and will gather you out of the countries wherein ye are scattered, with a mighty hand, and with a stretched out arm, and with fury poured out . . . And I will bring you into the wilderness of the people, and there will I plead with you face to face . . . And I will cause you to pass under the rod, and I will

The result of the judgment of Israel will be the conversion of Israel as a nation at the Second Coming of Christ.

bring you into the bond of the covenant: And I will purge out from among you the rebels, and them that transgress against me: I will bring them forth out of the country where they sojourn, and they shall not enter into the land of Israel: and ye shall know that I am the LORD . . . I will accept you with your sweet savour, when I bring you out from the people, and gather you out of the countries wherein ye have been scattered;

Jesus Christ in person, along with the resurrected saints of all ages, will reign on earth for a thousand years as He puts all enemies under His feet and re-establishes the universal kingdom of God.

and I will be sanctified in you before the heathen . . . And ye shall know that I am the LORD, when I have wrought with you for my name's sake, not according to your wicked ways, nor according to your corrupt doings, O ye house of Israel, saith the Lord GOD (Ezek. 20:33-44)

1. *Subjects*: The living Jews (Zech. 12: 10-15).
2. *Time*: During the Tribulation (Jer. 30:3-11; Mt. 24:15-22; Dan. 9:27).
3. *Place*: Palestine, Edom and Moab (Zech. 12:4-15; 13:1; 14:1-21; Dan. 11:40-45; Isa. 16:1-5; Ezek. 20:33-44; Hos. 2:14-17; Mt. 24:15-31; Rev. 12).
4. *Basis*: Obedience to God and His Word (Jas. 1:22-25).
5. *Result*: Conversion of Israel as a nation at the Second Coming of Christ (Rom. 11:25-29; Zech. 12:10–13:1; Ezek. 22:19-22; Jer. 30:3-11; Isa. 66:7, 8; Mt. 23:37-39).

VI. The Judgment of the Nations
(Mt. 25:31-46)

The judgment of the nations ends the Age of Grace—the age in which we now live—and begins the Millennium. This judgment will end the period of man's sinful rule on the earth. Jesus Christ in person, along with the resurrected saints of all ages, will reign on earth for a thousand years as He puts all enemies under His feet and re-establishes the universal kingdom of God. Once the kingdom of God is fully established, Christ will reign forever. This judgment will determine who is worthy of entrance into the kingdom of Heaven and who will be executed and cut off from entrance into the kingdom. Daniel's prophecy will then be fullfilled:

> Blessed is he that waiteth, and cometh to the thousand three hundred and five and thirty days (Dan. 12:12)

This is seventy-five days after the Battle of Armageddon. During this time the nations will be gathered and judged, the Jews will be regathered and settled in the land of promise, and all necessary preliminary arrangements for the kingdom will be made.

1. *Subjects*: Gentile nations (Mt. 25:32).
2. *Time*: At the revelation of Christ before the Millennium (Mt. 25:31-46).
3. *Place*: Palestine (Zech.14; Mt. 25:31; Rev. 19:11-21).
4. *Basis*: Their treatment of Christ's breth-

ren—the Jews (Mt. 25:31-46).

5. *Result*: Some saved to go into the Millennium and some destroyed (Mt. 25:34, 41, 46; Zech.14; Mt.13:41-50; 24:51; Isa. 53; Joel 3).

A comparison of Mt. 25:31-46 with Rev. 20:11-15 will reveal that this judgment is entirely different from the Great White Throne Judgment detailed in Point I. A few points of contrast are as follows:

Judgment of the Nations vs. Great White Throne Judgment

Judgment of the Nations

1. Living nations (Mt. 25:31-46)
2. Before the Millennium (Mt. 25:41-46)
3. Christ the judge (Mt. 25:31)
4. On earth (Mt. 25:31-46; Zech. 14)
5. Two classes (Mt. 25:31-46)
6. Some saved (Mt. 25:34; Zech. 14:16)
7. Some destroyed (Mt. 25:41-46)
8. No resurrection (Mt. 25:32; Zech. 14)
9. No books opened (Mt. 25:31-46)

10. Basis: sins, especially one sin—persecution of Israel (Mt. 25:31-46)
11. One generation (Mt. 25:31-46)
12. Gentiles only (Mt. 25:32)
13. Angels help in this judgment (Mt. 13:42-50; 24:31; 25:31)

Great White Throne Judgment

1. Wicked dead resurrected (Rev. 20:11-15)
2. After the Millennium (Rev. 20:1-15)
3. God the judge (Rev. 20:11-15)
4. In Heaven (Rev. 20:11-15)
5. One class (Rev. 20:11-15)
6. None saved (Rev. 20:4-15)
7. All destroyed (Rev. 20:4-15)
8. A resurrection (Rev. 20:4-15)
9. Books opened (Rev. 20:11-15)
10. Sins of all the ages recorded in the books (Rev. 20:11-15)
11. All generations (Rev. 20:11-15; Acts 17:31)
12. Jews and Gentiles (Rev. 20:11-15; Acts 17:31)
13. No angels mentioned at this judgment.

VII. The Judgment of Angels
(2 Pet. 2:4; Jude 6, 7)

> For if God spared not the angels
> that sinned, but cast them down
> to hell, and delivered them
> into chains of darkness, to be
> reserved unto judgment (2 Pet.
> 2:4)

1. *Subjects*: Fallen angels (2 Pet. 2:4; Jude 6, 7).
2. *Time*: After the Millennium (2 Pet. 2:4; Jude 6, 7; Rev. 20:7-15).
3. *Place*: In Heaven (Rev. 20:12).
4. *Basis*: Sins (2 Pet. 2:4; Jude 6, 7).
5. *Result*: Eternal damnation in the Lake of Fire (Rev. 20:10; Mt. 25:41).

Satan and demons will perhaps be judged at the same time (Eph. 6:12; Mk. 8:28; Lk. 8:31).

Chapter Two

BIBLICAL STUDIES

I. THE BIBLE IS EASY TO UNDERSTAND

The Bible is a simple book to understand. We've seen that as we've studied a topic that many consider complex and obscure. Even biblical prophecy, an area of Scripture that many assume to be beyond comprehension, is as easy to understand as the accounts of Jonah, Daniel or Joseph. This probably sounds ridiculous to most people, but perhaps considering a few simple facts will change your mind! Consider the following points:

The Bible Is a Revelation. The Bible is an inspired revelation from God. A revelation is an uncovering or unveiling so that everyone may see what was previously covered or hidden.

The Bible Contains Many Repeated Truths. Over and over the Bible repeats truth so that

40

"in the mouth of two or three witnesses every word may be established" (Dt. 17:6-7; 19:15; Mt. 18:16; 2 Cor. 13:1; 1 Tim. 5:19; Heb. 10: 28). Because of this fact, any doctrine that is not plainly stated in Scripture is best left alone. When God says something about a particular topic, it will be found repeated in several places, so we will not be left in doubt as to what God says. Our part is to collect everything God says on a subject—making it so clear that no interpretation is necessary. If we do this, nothing will need to be added to or taken from the Bible in order to understand the truth. All we need to do is to find out where "it is written" and then believe it. We must always make our ideas conform to the Bible and not the Scripture to our ideas.

> *All we need to do is to find out where "it is written" and then believe it. We must always make our ideas conform to the Bible and not the Scripture to our ideas.*

The Bible is Written in Simple Language. It is intended to be read and understood without interpretation. All God considers necessary

41

to understand the Bible is childlike faith. God made both man and His Word, and they fit together as a lock and key (Job 32:8; 38:3-6; Jn. 1:4-9). Even the ungodly can understand, if they so desire (Rom. 1:16-20).

The Bible is a Simple Book to Understand Because Most of it is Either History or Simple Instructions about How to Live. About 25,007 verses of the Bible—about 80 percent of it—contain simple history, commands, warnings, promises, rebukes, and plain instructions by means of which men may understand the will of God. The remaining 20 percent (or 6,207 verses) are prophecy written in the same simple human language that is used to record history. Of these 6,207 prophetic verses, 3,299 have been fulfilled and are now history. The 2,908 other verses are unfulfilled prophecy.

> *God made both man and His Word, and they fit together as a lock and key. Even the ungodly can understand, if they so desire.*

II. DEFINITION OF TERMS

It is important to define some of the important terms we'll be using in this book:

INTERPRET: To state the true sense of God's message as He expresses it; that is, give to the reader the exact statements of Scripture without change; to state exactly what God says and where He says it.

HERMENEUTICS is the science or art of interpretation and explanation. It comes from the Greek *hermeneuo*, meaning "to explain," "to expound," and "to interpret" (Jn. 1:38-42; 9:7; Heb. 7:2). It is the science which establishes and classifies the principles, methods, and rules by which the meaning of the author's language is ascertained. The interpretation of any piece of literature will depend upon the nature of the work under consideration. Poetry, history, fiction, and other forms of human expression require a different set of rules. The rules that govern the writing of fiction would not be suitable for historical prose. Accordingly, the rules that govern biblical interpretation depend upon the character of its separate kinds of writings, just as is true of different kinds of writings in other books.

Since the Bible is like other books in that it is written in human language, it must be interpreted like all other literature. If heavenly, supernatural, and spiritual truths are written in human language, we must understand such

> *There can be no special biblical logic, rhetoric, or grammar. The laws of grammar apply to the Bible as they do to other writings.*

truths on this basis. The words and expressions found in the Bible must be understood in the same manner as words and expressions found outside of it. There can be no special biblical logic, rhetoric, or grammar. The laws of grammar apply to the Bible as they do to other writings.

BIBLICAL HERMENEUTICS is the science which establishes and classifies the principles, methods, and rules by which the Word of God is made plain.

EXEGESIS is the application of the rules of biblical hermeneutics to the unfolding of the meaning of a passage of Scripture. Interpretation expresses exactly the mind and thoughts of another and is purely a reproductive process, involving no originality of thought on the part of the interpreter. Exegesis is the use of the science of interpretation in the reproduction of the thoughts of God as expressed in Scripture.

III. THE TRUE METHOD OF BIBLE INTERPRETATION

The fundamental principle is to gather from the Scriptures themselves the precise meaning the writers intended to convey. It applies to the Bible the same principles, rules, grammatical process, and exercise of common sense and reason that we apply to other books. In doing this, one must take the Bible literally when it is at all possible. When a statement is found that cannot possibly be literal, as Jesus being a "door" or of a woman being clothed with the sun and standing on the moon and on her head a crown of twelve stars, or of land animals coming out of the sea, and other statements which are obviously not literal, then we know the language is figurative. In such cases we must get the literal truth conveyed by the figurative language, and the truth intended to be conveyed will be as literal as if it were expressed in literal language without the use of such figures. After all, figurative language expresses literal truth as much as if such figures were not used. In a general sense, the true method of Bible interpretation embraces the following ideas:

Interpretation expresses exactly the mind and thoughts of another and is purely a reproductive process, involving no originality of thought on the part of the interpreter. Exegesis is the use of the science of interpretation in the reproduction of the thoughts of God as expressed in Scripture.

1. The primary meaning of words and their common use in a particular age in which they are used, and the importance of synonyms.

2. The grammatical construction and idiomatic peculiarities of the languages of the Bible, and the meaning of the context, both immediate and remote.

3. Comparison of parallel passages on the same subject.

4. The purpose or object of each writer in each particular book.

5. The historical background of each writer and the circumstances under which he wrote.

6. The general plan of the entire Bible, and its moral and spiritual teachings.

7. The agreement of Scripture in its several parts, and its prophecies and their fulfillment.

8. The manners and customs of the particular age and land of each writer.

9. Understanding of how to interpret prophecy, poetry, allegories, symbols, parables, figures of speech, types, and all other forms of human expression.

When all these facts are kept in mind by the student, and all scriptures interpreted in harmony with all these principles, there cannot possibly be any misunderstanding of any part of the Bible.

IV. GENERAL RULES OF BIBLE INTERPRETATION

1.   The entire Bible came from God and possesses unity of design and teaching. We shall, therefore, consider both Testaments together as being equally inspired.

2.   It may be assumed that no one resorts to speech or writing without having some idea to express; that in order to express that idea he will use words and forms of speech familiar to his hearers or readers; and that if he uses a word or figure of speech in a different sense from what is commonly understood he will make the fact known.

3.   The Bible cannot contradict itself. Its teachings in one part must agree with its teachings in another part. Therefore, any interpretation which makes the Bible inconsistent with itself must rest upon false principles.

4.   No meaning should be gleaned from the Bible except that which a fair and honest, grammatical, and historical interpretation yields.

5.   Language is an accumulation of words used to interchange thoughts. To understand the language of the speaker or writer, it is necessary to know the meaning of his words. A true meaning of the words is a true meaning of the sense. It is as true of the Bible as of any other book.

> *The Bible cannot contradict itself. Its teachings in one part must agree with its teachings in another part. Therefore, any interpretation which makes the Bible inconsistent with itself must rest upon false principles.*

6.   Often to fully understand a passage of Scripture, the scope or plan of the entire book must be known. Sometimes the design of the books are made clear, as in the case of Proverbs (1:1-4); Isaiah (1:1-3); John (20:31); Revelation (1:1); etc. If the definite purpose of the book is not stated, the purpose of the book must be

gotten from the contents and from the design of the Bible as a whole, as is clear in Jn. 5: 39; 2 Tim. 2:15; 3:16-17. Some seeming contradictions are cleared up when this rule is observed. The difference between Paul and James is easily understood when the design of their books is understood and recognized. In Romans, Paul seeks to prove that a man is not saved by works, while in James he seeks to show that a man cannot remain saved unless he brings forth good works.

> *The difference between Paul and James is easily understood when the design of their books is understood and recognized. In Romans, Paul seeks to prove that a man is not saved by works, while in James he seeks to show that a man cannot remain saved unless he brings forth good works.*

7.   Sometimes the connection is obscured through the use of virtual dialogue between the writers and unseen persons, as in Ps. 15; Isa. 52:13; 63:1-6; Rom. 3; etc.

8.   One of the most fundamental rules of

interpretation is that of comparing Scripture with Scripture. It is by a strict and honest observance of this rule that the true meaning can be gotten when every other thing has failed to make clear the meaning. Before arriving at the whole truth, be sure that all the scriptures on a subject are collected together and read at one time. If there is any question left after you have done this, then go over the whole subject carefully until every question is cleared up.

> *In some places a statement on a subject may be very brief and seemingly obscure and will be made perfectly clear by a larger passage on the same subject. Always explain the seemingly difficult with the more simple scriptures.*

9.   In some places a statement on a subject may be very brief and seemingly obscure and will be made perfectly clear by a larger passage on the same subject. Always explain the seemingly difficult with the more simple scriptures. No doctrine founded upon a single verse of Scripture contains the whole of the subject; so do not be dishonest and wrest with Scripture or force a meaning into a

passage that is not clearly understood in the passage or in parallel passages on the same subject.

10. The progressive character of revelation and the gradual development of truth should be recognized. Some truths found in germ in the Old Testament are fully developed in the New Testament. For example, the idea of blood sacrifices was developed from the time of Abel until it was fully culminated and made eternally clear in the sacrifice of Christ on Calvary.

> *Water baptism, the Lord's Supper, and other New Testament doctrines are not found in the Old Testament at all. It is not proper to ask whether David was baptized in water, or whether Saul was a Christian, because these are New Testament terms.*

11. The meaning of a word or phrase in the New Testament must not be carried back into Old Testament doctrine unless such is warranted by both Testaments. For example, water baptism, the Lord's Supper, and other New Testament doctrines are not found in the Old Testament

at all. It is not proper to ask whether David was baptized in water, or whether Saul was a Christian, because these are New Testament terms.

12. Passages obviously literal should not be spiritualized. For example, making the natural blessings of Canaan the spiritual blessings of Heaven; regarding the ark of Noah as salvation through Christ, and hundreds of like interpretations.

13. The dispensational character of Scripture should be noted so that one can pigeon-hole every passage of Scripture in some definite period in God's plan.

14. The three classes of people (the Jews, the Church, and the Gentiles) dealt with in Scripture should be noted. Up to Genesis 12, the race as a whole is dealt with. From Gen. 12 to the New Testament the Jews and the Gentiles are dealt with; and in the New Testament these and the Church of God, made up of Jews and Gentiles, are dealt with (1 Cor. 10:32).

15.   In the study of doctrine, the practical aspect must be kept in view (2 Tim. 3:16-17).

16.   The comparative importance of truth should be emphasized. The positive truths should be studied more than the negative. It is more important to have faith instead of unbelief; to know God better than Satan, etc. So, one should learn more about faith and God than unbelief and Satan.

> *The comparative importance of truth should be empha-sized. The positive truths should be studied more than the negative. It is more important to have faith instead of unbelief; to know God better than Satan.*

17.   General famil-iarity with the Bible as a whole is very important. Keep reading the Bible over and over until its contents as a whole are familiar. The more one can remember here and there what he has read, the clearer the Bible will become.

18.   Words of Scripture must agree with the content and the subject matter in the pas-sages where found. No meaning should be given to a word that would be in the least out

of harmony with any scripture. For example, the word "seen" in John 1:18 should be understood to mean "comprehended" in order to harmonize with all scriptures that state men saw God with the natural eyes.

19. Careful attention should be paid to connecting words that connect events with each other, as the words "when," "then," etc., in Mt. 24:15-16, 21, 23, 40; 25:1.

> Ascertain the exact meaning of the words of Scripture. The way a word is used, the subject matter, and the context often determine the true meaning.

20. Careful attention should be paid to prepositions, definite articles, names of different persons and places with the same name, same persons and places with different names, and the names of different persons and places that are spelled differently by different authors in different books.

21. Ascertain the exact meaning of the words of Scripture. The way a word is used, the subject matter, and the context often determine the true meaning.

22.   Hebrew and Greek idioms should be noted. Sometimes a person having a peculiar characteristic, or subject to a peculiar evil, or destined to a particular destiny is called the child of that evil or destiny (Lk. 10:6; Eph. 2:1-3; 2 Thess. 2:3). The word "father" is applied to the originator of any custom or to the inventor of something (Gen. 4:20-21; Jn. 8:44). It is also used for "ancestor" (1 Chr. 1:17). The words "son" and "daughter" are sometimes used of descendants or in–laws (Gen. 46:22; Lk. 3:23). The words "brother" and "cousin" are sometimes used of relatives and countrymen (Gen. 14:16 with 11:31; Lk. 1:36, 58). Names of parents are used of posterity (1 Ki. 18:17-18).

> *Ascertain the exact meaning of the words of Scripture. The way a word is used, the subject matter, and the context often determine the true meaning.*

23.   Preference is sometimes expressed by the word "hate" (Lk. 14:26; Rom. 9:13).

24.   A peculiar idiom concerning numbers must be understood. Sometimes round num-

bers rather than the exact number are used (Jdg. 20:35, 46). This will explain seeming contradictions between numbers. Failure to understand this idiom may have caused copyists and translators to misunderstand the numbers of some passages which seem erroneous and very large. For example, in 1 Sam. 6:19, we read the Lord smote in a very small town 50,070 people, which, in the Hebrew text reads, "seventy men two fifties and one thousand" or 70–100–1,000, or 1,170 people.

25. Careful attention should be paid to parenthesis, the use of italics (meaning these words are not in the original but supplied in English to make sense), the use of capital letters, marginal notes, references, summaries of chapters, chapter and page headings, the division of the text into chapters and verses, punctuation, obsolete English words, the rendering of the same original words by different English words, and other things about the English translations. All these things are human additions to the original text and should not be relied upon. For example, the

running of references to prove a doctrine is sometimes misleading. The references may not be on the same subject, as can be easily detected by the reader.

26. Seeming contradictions in Scripture should be considered in the light of all the principles stated above. It must be kept in mind that the Bible records sayings of men under pressure of trials who said things that they never would have said otherwise. It records sayings of backsliders and rebels against God. It records statements of Satan and demons, and the words of such rebels should never be taken as the words from the mouth of God. They should not always be held as truth, for sometimes they are lies. Inspiration guarantees that these rebels said those things, but it does not guarantee that what they said is truth. Sometimes such statements contradict those of God and good men under divine utterance. Enemies of God take such contradictions between what God says and what rebels against God say and use them to prove the Bible contradicts itself. Naturally, such contradictions are found in

the Bible, but they are not contradictions between statements made by God. The only statements that can be relied upon as truth are those that come from God and men who speak for God as the Spirit gives utterance, and in these there is no contradiction.

The Bible records sayings of men under pressure of trials who said things that they never would have said otherwise. It records sayings of backsliders and rebels against God. It records statements of Satan and demons, and the words of such rebels should never be taken as the words from the mouth of God.

The Bible also records the changes of God's will and plan in a later age over that of an earlier one. Such changes have been taken by the ungodly as contradictions, but such have had to be made by God because of the sin and rebellion of the people to whom He promised such things and for whom He made a certain plan. For example, in Gen. 1:31 God saw everything that He had made and it was good, but in Gen. 6:6 God repented that He had made man. In the meantime, between the two passages, sin and rebellion had entered, which made it necessary for God to have a changed attitude toward man. God has had to change his plan temporarily because of man's sin, but the original and eternal plan of God for creation has never been changed and never will be. God will finally realize His original purpose; that is the reason for His present dispensational dealings. God deals with each generation as circumstances demand. Sometimes God has had to change His promises to a certain group

The seeming contradictions between the sermons of Mt. 5 and Lk. 6 are cleared up when we see that there were two sermons—one on the mount and the other "in the plain." The so-called contradictions of the Bible are unreal and imaginary.

because they refused to meet the conditions for the fulfillment of these promises.

27. The seeming contradictions in the New Testament will also vanish and be cleared up if men would be as fair with God as they will want God to be with them in the judgment. Always look for an explanation

and it will be found. For example, men criticize the Bible for lack of harmony between the temptations of Christ in Mt. 4, and those in Lk. 4. But when we consider the fact that there were two separate sets of temptations during the forty days, and that after the first set of tests in Luke, Satan was dismissed "for a season," and after the last set of tests in Matthew, Satan was dismissed for good, there is no contradiction. The seeming contradictions between the sermons of Mt. 5 and Lk. 6 are cleared up when we see that there were two sermons—one on the mount and the other "in the plain." The so-called contradictions of the Bible are unreal and imaginary. Because of the lack of information as to the time, places, circumstances, etc., men cannot always judge concerning them. So it would be best always to give God the benefit of the doubt, since He knows all things and was there when things happened. If He did not see fit to give all details so as to make every small detail clear, that is His wisdom. It should not detract from faith in God and His revelation.

All seeming contradictions in the Bible are easily cleared up with a better knowledge of the text, by correct translation, by knowing the manners and customs of the age and the country in which the books were written, by a wider application of historical facts, and by a fair and sane application of the rules of interpretation given above.

Chapter Three

PROPHECY

How to Interpret Prophecy

As we have undertaken this study of prophecy, we've followed a few basic principles. It is important that we learn some general rules of biblical interpretation as we continue to study the Scriptures. Many preachers and Bible teachers make the statement that prophecy is hard to understand. Actually, biblical prophecy is pretty simple to understand—it's the attempt to harmonize the rampant speculation and various interpretations that's difficult! Thankfully, the Bible is easy to understand if one will follow a few common–sense rules:

(1) Grant the same meaning to the words of prophecy that are given to words of history; that is, give the same meaning to the words of the entire Bible that are given to the same

words outside the Bible. It's a common misconception that just because a word is found in a prophetic passage, or because it is in the Bible, it must have a mystical meaning and cannot be understood in the literal sense. For example, the word "year" is generally understood (wrongly!) to mean a day, and a day to mean a year, just because it is prophecy.

(2) Do not change the literal to a spiritual or symbolic meaning.

One author, in his book of lectures on Revelation, is a fair example of the current trend of changing words and statements away from their literal meaning to any meaning that suits one's fancy. This particular author interprets the word "earthquake" of the sixth seal (Rev. 6:12-17) to be the breaking up of society instead of a literal earthquake; the sun darkened to be a type of Christ rejected and God dethroned; the moon turned to blood to be the destruction of derived authority; the stars falling to be the downfall and apostasy of religious leaders in the ecclesiastical heavens (whatever they are); and the heavens departing as a scroll to be that all organized Christianity will be destroyed.

This same writer also claims that the trumpet judgments, found in Revelation 8, are not to be interpreted literally as well. In his view, the grass of the first trumpet (Rev. 8:7) refers to the "common people" and the trees refer to the dignity of man, so instead of the grass and one–third of the trees being literally burned, as is plainly stated, all common men and one–third of man's dignity will be burned.

Instead of a third of the sea being turned to blood, a third of the creatures dying, and a third of the ships being destroyed in the second trumpet (Rev. 8:8, 9), the burning mountain causing this, he says, means spiritual Babylon cast into the

> *The common theory that just because a word is found in prophecy, or because it is in the Bible, it automatically has a mystical meaning and cannot be understood in the literal sense is entirely wrong. For example, the word "year" is generally taken to mean a day and a day to mean a year just because it is prophecy.*

sea of nations and destroyed by the people.

This author further states that instead of the drinking waters being made bitter by a star falling from Heaven, which causes the death of many men as in the third trumpet (Rev. 8:10, 11), the star falling from Heaven means the pope of Rome or some religious dignitary. But how could the pope fall from Heaven into the waters and poison them? And how could he poison the drinking waters if he did fall into them?

The darkening of a third of the sun, moon, and stars as in the fourth trumpet (Rev. 8:12), he says, means spiritual darkness instead of the literal darkening of part of the earth.

This writer explains the fifth trumpet (Rev. 9:1-12) as follows, "the star that falls from Heaven with the key to the Abyss is the pope or the apostate religious leader of the third trumpet. (This would make the pope fall from Heaven twice, once under the third trumpet and once again under the fifth trumpet.) The key is the system that opens the Abyss. The smoke of the pit is the blotting out of the true light in man's spiritual sky by demonic powers, when false religions are dominant after the Holy Spirit is taken out of the world. The locusts are not literal—they symbolize these false religions spreading like locusts. The torment of the stings of these creatures is the torment that these religions will bring. The faces of men that these creatures have means intelligence and reason (but since they are not real creatures how are they to exercise these faculties?). Their hair like women means an

> *The five months these creatures torment men are not literal and it is not explained what they mean. Thus nothing in Revelation is literal if we believe this method of interpretation.*

unholy life and the iron breastplates mean that the conscience is destroyed. The grass and the trees are not symbolic as they are in the first trumpet. The five months these creatures torment men are not literal and it is not explained what they mean. Thus, nothing in Revelation is literal if we believe this method of interpretation.

The sixth trumpet (Rev. 9:13-21), he says,

is not literal, but the 200,000,000 creatures refer to Asiatic hordes that overran Europe and Palestine through many centuries.

This writer says the two witnesses are not two men, but symbolize the witnessing Jewish remnant. He also says the manchild is Christ; the woman is Israel; the sun is the glory of the New Testaments; the moon the glory of the Old Testament; the twelve stars the twelve tribes; the 1,260 days of Rev. 12:6 mean the first part of Daniel's Seventieth Week when the woman flees, or Israel is scattered among the nations; the "times" of Rev. 12:14 refer to the last half of the Week; and the water the dragon casts out of his mouth is evil teaching, but Israel will escape these teachings and be the only testimony for God.

The key is the system that opens the Abyss. The smoke of the pit is the blotting out of the true light in man's spiritual sky by demon powers, when false religions are dominant after the Holy Spirit is taken out of the world.

He says the beast of Rev. 13 is the Revived Roman Empire, the seven heads are seven hills on which the city of Rome is built, the head wounded to death is imperial Rome Revived, but how could one of these literal hills be imperial Rome to be revived if it is part of the ground on which Rome is built?

He says the seven vials (Rev. 16:2-21) are not literal, except the fourth and fifth ones, but who is he to decide for us that these are the only judgments of the seals, trumpets, and vials that are literal? He explains the sores of the first vial as a spiritual plague, the second and third vials are the drying up of the source of life (whatever that means), and are not the sea and rivers literally turned to blood as it reads. The sixth vial is the destruction of the Turkish Empire instead of the literal drying up of the river Euphrates, but why not give

This method of interpretation of Revelation really should be called "How not to interpret prophecy," for it does away with the literal meaning of God's own revelation and substitutes man's theories instead.

69

this river the same meaning as in Gen. 2:14; 15:18; Jer. 13:4-7; 46:2-10; 51:63; Rev. 9:14, and see how ridiculous it would be? He says that the "earthquake" of the seventh vial that destroys the city of Babylon and many cities of the nations is not literal. It means the destruction of every religious institution and civilization as we now know it today.

This method of interpretation of Revelation really should be called "How *not* to interpret prophecy," for it completely does away with the literal meaning of God's own revelation and substitutes man's theories instead. If these ideas are really what God wanted revealed, could not

> *Be satisfied with what God has seen fit to reveal and never read between the lines or add to Scripture in order to understand it.*

God have made this clear when He gave the Revelation, instead of giving us what He did reveal? Would He have to wait until this author lived to find the "real" truth of prophetic statements?

(3) Do not seek to find hidden meanings in

the words of Scripture, or add to Scripture. Be satisfied with what God has seen fit to reveal and never read between the lines or add to Scripture in order to understand it. For example, elaborate schemes have been developed to determine if historical figures could have been the Antichrist. Their names have been transliterated into Greek to see if their they equal "666." This is all foolish speculation and proves nothing concerning the mark or the name of the Antichrist, as we shall see.

Others find the United States in prophecy by taking the letters U. S. A. out of the name Jer-USA-lem. If this is the only way we can find the United States in prophecy, it would be best to leave her out. The fact is that the United States is not once mentioned in prophecy anywhere. Isaiah 18 refers to the inhabitants of the Sudan "which is beyond the rivers of Ethiopia" and it does not refer to the United States. The white horse rider of Rev. 6 and the False Prophet of Rev. 13:11-18; 19:20; 20:10, do not refer to the United States.

Still others find the mark of the Beast in the faces on the American dime, in keeping Sunday as the sabbath, in union cards, in social security numbers, in rationing, and

---

The Mark of the Beast:

Did you know that the mark of the Beast is not 666? This is the "number of the beast" and not his mark, as is plainly stated in Rev. 13:16-18. There will be three things men will have a choice of taking in the days of Antichrist: The mark of Antichrist, his name, or the number of his name. What the Antichrist's name and mark will be is not stated; but the number of his name is stated as being 666. Therefore, no one can know his name or his mark and we won't know them until the Antichrist comes after the rapture of the Church. However, anyone now can know that 666 is the number of his name, as this is revealed in Rev. 13:18.

---

in many other ridiculous theories. These and many other prophetic interpretations are preached on Sundays and written in popular novels. Believers, naturally, spread these foolish theories as truth, relying on the authority of the pulpit and the written word instead of the Word of God. The devil stands back and laughs at such foolish speculation and distortion of God's Word, for he knows that the confusion being spread by the large variety of contradictory teachings causes many to discard prophecy altogether as they become skeptical about the real truth when they do hear it.

Still others find the mark of the Beast in the faces on the American dime, in keeping Sunday as the sabbath, in union cards, in social security numbers, in rationing, and many other ridiculous theories.

(4) Believe that prophecy can be understood just as it is, without any changes or additions, and that it is simply a record of things to happen at some time after its utterance. Prophecy should be understood as literally as history. After all, history is

simply a record of what has happened and prophecy is a record of what is going to happen. Both kinds of records are written in the same everyday language and both should be understood on the same basis. God expects us to understand both just as they are written, and He will judge us for not using our common intelligence to understand both as they are plainly written.

(5) We should forget the idea that prophecy must be fulfilled before it can be understood. If we can only understand prophecy in hindsight, then it has failed in its purpose of revealing to us beforehand what is to happen. Many authors apologize for their uncertainty concerning the things of which they write and declare that we cannot hope to fully understand prophecies until their final fulfillment. It would be better not to write at all, than to be uncertain about what is being written. There is no need for uncertainty, or apology, if one is relying on Scripture to interpret itself, rather than on one's own interpretations.

What we mean to emphasize by this point is that all true prophecy is clear in its description of future events, and it is just as clear before it happens as it is after it is fulfilled.

Let's take a look at one example—modern inventions as a fulfillment of prophecy. No one had interpreted Nahum 2:3, 4 in connection with an automobile until they were invented. Men never dreamed of airplanes, radios, locomotives, or any other man–made invention, and they never interpreted any Scripture as predicting them until after they were invented. But following their invention, students of prophecy

> *Prophecy should be understood as literally as history. After all, history is simply a record of what has happened and prophecy is a record of what is going to happen. Both kinds of records are written in the same everyday language and both should be understood on the same basis.*

soon claimed they found them in prophetic passages from Genesis to Revelation. Prior to 1945, Bible students never dreamed of atomic bombs as a subject of prophecy, but immediately after they were dropped in that year, prophetic sensationalists arose from their long slumber and ignorance and found them in Scripture. Thus, in a short period of time, nearly everyone in Christendom (if sensationalists are believed), knew that the atom bomb was a fulfillment of several prophecies! The world is coming to an end, and many other prophecies will be fulfilled by the atom bomb, or so these students of prophecy have stated.

The sooner that we all have our speculative, sensational, prophetic appendix removed, the better off we will be, and the sooner the good name of prophecy will be restored, and men will again respect true prophecy as stated by God. The fact is that no invention is mentioned in particular in the Bible. The so–called automobile in Nahum 2:3, 4 refers to horse–drawn chariots of the king of Nineveh and those of Nebuchadnezzar in actual combat in the streets of Nineveh over the possession of the Assyrian Empire. This fact is made clear in Nahum 2:1-4, 13; 3:1-3, where we have mention of "the whip . .

. rattling of the wheels, and of the prancing horses" and "the horsemen." The so—called locomotive of Job 41 is "king over all the children of pride," according to the last verse. The phrase "as birds flying" in Isaiah 31:5 does not refer to the airplane but to the Second Coming of Christ as is proven in the passage itself. It states that "as birds flying" God, not airplanes, will come down to fight for Israel, and at that time every man shall cast away his idols forever. We all know that this did not happen in 1917 when General Allenby took Jerusalem from the Turks. No, this prophecy will be fulfilled when the armies of Heaven come with Jesus "as birds flying" as in Zech. 14:

Prior to 1945, Bible students never dreamed of atom bombs as a subject of prophecy, but immediately after they were dropped in that year, prophetic sensationalists arose from their long slumber and ignorance and found them in prophecy. Thus, in a short period of time, nearly everyone in Christendom (if sensationalists are believed), knew that the atom bomb was a fulfillment of several prophecies!

1-5; 2 Thess. 1:7-10; Jude 14; Rev. 19:11-21; etc. And so it goes with all of the man–made inventions that some find in prophetic passages. The context always proves that the subject of the passage is not some modern invention. Daniel 12:4 is the only verse in the entire Bible that covers modern inventions, at least in general terms. Still, one can preach from this verse without sensationalism or speculation.

> *God, not airplanes, will come down to fight for Israel, and at that time every man shall cast away his idols forever, and we all know that this did not happen in 1917 when General Allenby took Jerusalem from the Turks.*

(6) Do not interpret God's own explanation of any symbol or prophecy or change God's meaning from that which is plainly and obviously clear. God always interprets His own symbols as can be seen in Dan. 2: 38-44; 7:17, 23-26; 8:20-23; 9:20-27; 11: 2-45; 12:1-13; Rev. 1:20; 12:9; 13:18; 17: 8-18; etc. Clear, literal prophecy needs no interpretation as it is simply history written before it happens. If God uses a word or a

figure of speech (or any other form of human expression) in a different way from that which is commonly understood, we have a right to expect Him to make due explanation. Otherwise, we should view His Word as it is commonly used and understood. When there is no explanation of a symbol or a figure of speech it is to be taken for granted that it is not only clear in itself, but it is clear from its usage elsewhere in Scripture, and especially when it is harmonized with all other scriptures on the same subject.

(7) Give only one meaning to a passage—the plain literal meaning—unless it is made clear that a double meaning should be understood. In order to understand certain prophecies there are two laws that should be followed.

A. *The law of double reference.* In some passages two distinct persons are referred to, the visible person addressed and the invisible person who is using the visible one as a tool.

B. *The law of prophetic perspective.* This

79

law is that of recording future events as if they were continuous and successive, when there may be thousands of years between the events. For example, in Isa. 61:1-3, as recorded in Lk. 4:17-20, Christ stopped His reading in the prophecy at the words "the acceptable year of the Lord." He closed the book and said, "This day is this scripture fulfilled in your ears." If He had continued reading the prophecy and had said, "and the day of vengeance of our God,"—and had said this was fulfilled that day—His statement would have been untrue, for "the day of vengeance" has not yet come. There have been already about two thousand years since "the acceptable year of the Lord." The day of vengeance has not yet come, and will not come until the future Tribulation. Both events are in one verse in the prophecy and have only a comma between them. While this would seem to indicate that since both events were given together they would follow each other in succession, they did not.

In other words, the prophets see things in the same vision as one would look at a distant range of mountain peaks where the valleys between them are not seen. One must learn to look at every prophetic event and collect together all that is said about that particular event in both the Old and New Testaments. Then, we see when it will be fulfilled in connection with the other events. This is rightly dividing the Word of Truth (2 Tim. 2:15).

> The fact is that there may be thousands of years between the events. For example, in Isa. 61:1-3, as recorded in Lk. 4:17-20, Christ stopped His reading in the prophecy at the words "the acceptable year of the Lord." He closed the book and said, "This day is this scripture fulfilled in your ears."

(8) The key to the interpretation of many prophecies is to regard the prophet primarily as a preacher of righteousness. A prophet was not only a foreteller but a forthteller. He was a speaker for God, to rebuke, to instruct, and to correct people in his day, as well as to foretell future events. He had powers of insight and foresight and he was more than a

foreteller of future events. He was inspired to see conditions around him and the purposes of God in these things. The present was only a moment in the divine plan which was working toward the end of establishing the kingdom of God again on earth and ridding the earth of all rebellion. Hence, the prophet was a teacher, a social reformer, and a statesman, as well as a herald of the future kingdom. Many of his utterances

One thing to keep in mind when dealing with prophecy is the history of the writer and his times and the circumstances under which he wrote.

were really sermons preached as the occasion demanded. This is especially true of Isaiah, Jeremiah, Ezekiel, and the Minor Prophets, although in their books there are many prophecies of the future. Daniel and John were mainly prophets for foretelling future events, although in their books there is the element of forthtelling as seen in Daniel 2, 4, 5, 6, and Revelation 2, 3.

(9) One thing to keep in mind when dealing with prophecy is the history of the writer

and his times and the circumstances under which he wrote. One must understand the exact position of the writer as to the age in which he lived and the purpose of his predictions, the people to whom he wrote and the subject of his message. With a knowledge of the historical background, the manners and customs of the age and of people to whom he wrote, the peculiar idioms and human expressions of his times, and the purpose he had in view, one can avoid misunderstanding the intent of the biblical authors and of God Himself.

Chapter Four

THE IMPORTANCE OF FAITH

The Bible definitely declares that faith is all–important:

> But without faith it is impossible to please him: for he that cometh to God must believe that he is, and that he is a rewarder of them that diligently seek him (Heb. 11:6)

> Now faith is the substance of things hoped for, the evidence of things not seen (Heb. 11:1)

> But let him ask in faith, nothing wavering. For he that wavereth is like a wave of the sea driven with the wind and tossed. For let not that man think that he shall receive any thing of the Lord (Jas. 1:5-8)

> Whatsoever is not of faith is sin (Rom. 14:23)

Above all, taking the shield of faith, wherewith ye may be able to quench all the fiery darts of the wicked (Eph. 6:16)

Cast not away therefore your confidence, which hath great recompense of reward . . . Now the just shall LIVE BY FAITH: but if any man draw back, my soul shall have no pleasure in him (Heb. 10:35-39)

These scriptures, which clearly set forth the importance of faith, need no interpretation. They are clearly promises for us all.

And all things, whatsoever ye shall ask in prayer, believing ye shall receive (Matt. 21:21)

If thou canst believe, all things are possible to him that believeth (Mk. 9:23)

Have faith in God. For verily I say unto you, That whosoever shall say unto this mountain, Be thou removed, and be thou cast into the sea, and shall not doubt

85

in his heart, but shall believe
that those things which he saith
shall come to pass; he shall have
whatsoever he saith. Therefore, I
say unto you, What things soever
ye desire, when ye pray, believe
that ye receive them and ye shall
have them (Mk. 11:22-24)

These scriptures, which clearly set forth
the importance of faith, need no interpretation. They are clearly promises for us all—
that we can get whatsoever we have faith for.
In these verses we see no limitations or quali-
fications concerning known needs of this life
or the life to come; so we should impose our
own limits on God's promises. They are clear
in stating that faith is absolutely necessary to
obtain the things we desire. No one should
expect to receive anything from God if he
refuses to have faith. There is no such thing
as the impossibility of having faith, so the
fact that one does not have faith is his own
choice and responsibility. Jesus commanded
men to "Have faith in God," and such is possible, or it would not be mandatory.

It is all–important to have faith, because no prayer will be answered without it—God cannot be pleased without it; man will not get anything from God without it—and he will be disobedient to God without it. If faith is commanded, then not to have faith is to break the law of God and commit sin. If believers would realize this fact, they would become desperate about this law–breaking, as much as they are about breaking other laws of God. If we would only realize that it is sin to have unbelief and to doubt God, we would at least become moved to the point of action against such law–breaking.

There is no such thing as the impossibility of having faith, so the fact that one does not have faith is his own choice and responsibility. Jesus commanded men to "Have faith in God," and such is possible, or it would not be mandatory.

The trouble all along has been that most men consider unbelief and doubt to be a part of human nature—something to be expected and not to be changed. This attitude has been combined with a feeling of indifference.

87

During those times where life seems easy, when things are going well for us, there is no problem with the issue of faith. But when life becomes a struggle, and our faith falters, this lack of faith is shrugged off as something that cannot be helped. This is where the devil has the upper hand. The devil makes us think that not everyone can have a level of faith sufficient to obtain the promises of God, and that if one lacks faith, then it is perfectly right to live in unbelief.

> *Defeat is such a habit for the average Christian that he gives little thought to the possibility of victory. It is taken for granted, when the prayer is made, that there is little real chance that it will be answered. It is also assumed that the failure of God to grant an answer indicates that it is His will not to answer.*

If prayer is not answered, many believers take it for granted that it is not the will of God to grant an answer. They are quickly turned aside from their purpose and are satisfied with defeat. Blame for such defeat is laid upon God and the resulting circumstances are considered to be the will of God, while the truth is that this attitude is surrender to the devil and evil spirit–forces who oppose the answer to prayer. Defeat is such a habit for the average Christian that he gives little thought to the possibility of victory. It is taken for granted, when the prayer is offered up to God, that there is little real chance that it will be answered. Worse still, it is also assumed that the failure of God to grant an answer indicates that it is His will not to answer.

> *If our leaders would wage aggressive warfare against satanic forces, Satan would soon be defeated. If they would teach the truth as it is plainly written in Scripture, faith would soon be built up so that people would not take "no" for an answer to prayer.*

This condition in the lives of praying people has been created by wrong teaching in our churches for many years. Many who stand behind the pulpit will be quick to defend such failures and such teachings as being biblical. These teachings are largely to blame for our current condition of unbelief and our resignation to defeat in prayer. If our leaders would wage aggressive warfare against satanic forces, Satan would soon be defeated. If they would teach the truth as it is plainly written in Scripture, faith would soon be built up so that Christians would no longer take "no" for an answer to their prayers.

> *Unbelief is the sin that so easily overthrows the saints. It is not the major sins of the flesh that we permit to dominate us, but it is the sin of constantly doubting God. If none would doubt God there would be no failure to obtain an answer to prayer every time one prays for anything covered by the promises of God.*

Too many times such failures are seen as proof that it is not God's will to answer our prayers. The Word of God is entirely ignored as proof of anything. The failure to obtain an answer from God carries more weight in the lives of Christians than the Scriptures. However, the truth can be found by means of a diligent search of Scripture and the humility to acknowledge defeat to be the result of satanic and human sources. The truth is that because of unbelief and doubt, prayers remain unanswered and that such a result is never the true will of God.

> **Faith:**
>
> Faith is simple. It is believing God without wavering, doubting, or questioning what He says. It is taking God at His Word and believing that what He has promised He is able to perform. It is believing not only that He is able, but that He will do it. It is the quality of counting those things that "be not as though they were" (Rom. 4:17). Faith is also the absolute conviction that what God has promised and what we have asked according to His Word is already done. It is "the substance of things hoped for" and the first payment on things that we desire from God (Heb. 11:1-3).

Suppose God does not answer prayer; does this do away with His promises and make null and void His Word, or does it prove that man failed to have faith? What does the Bible say? If it says that God will always answer faith, then the lack of an answer simply shows unbelief. When the disciples asked Jesus, "Why could not we cast him out?" The answer was, "Because of your unbelief" (Matt. 17:14-21). Not one Scripture says that unanswered prayer indicates any other cause. When we try to excuse our unbelief and blame God for the failure, we sin against Him.

In Heb. 12:1-2 we are told,

> Wherefore seeing we also are compassed about with so great a cloud of witnesses, let us lay aside every weight, AND THE SIN which doth so easily beset us, and let us run with patience the race that is set before us. Looking unto Jesus the author and finisher of our faith.

Unbelief is the sin that so easily overthrows the saints. It is not the major sins of the flesh that we permit to dominate us, but it is the sin of constantly doubting God. If none would doubt God there would be no failure to obtain an answer to prayer every time one prays for anything covered by the promises of God.

GENERAL FACTS CONCERNING FAITH

FAITH CAN grow (2 Thess. 1:3), lead to utterance (2 Cor. 4:13), work through love (Gal. 5:6), clothe the naked (Matt. 6:30), heal the sick (Matt. 8:1-17; 9: 2, 22, 29; Jas. 5:14-16), dispel fear (Matt. 8:26), make whole (Mk. 10: 52), save from sin (Lk. 7:36-50; Eph. 2:8-9), fill believers (Acts 6:5-8), purify the heart (Acts 15: 9), sanctify (Acts 26:18), impart revelations (Rom. 1:17), justify (Rom. 3:28-31; Gal. 3:24), give access into grace (Rom.

Suppose God does not answer prayer; does this do away with His promises and make null and void His Word, or does it prove that man failed to have faith? What does the Bible say? If it says that God will always answer faith, then the lack of an answer simply shows unbelief.

5:2), produce righteousness (Rom. 9:30-32; 10:6-10; Phil. 3:9) and give security (Rom. 11:20; 2 Cor. 1:24).

FAITH CAN BRING blessings (Gal. 3:9), impart the Holy Spirit (Gal. 3:14), make men children of God (Gal. 3:26), bring hope and salvation (Gal. 5:5; Eph. 2:8-9), make conscious of Christ (Eph. 3:17), quench fiery darts of Satan (Eph. 6:16), produce works (Phil. 1:17; Jas. 2; 1 Thess. 1:3; 2 Thess. 1:11), edify (1 Tim. 1:4), produce inheritance (Heb. 6:12), and keep one true to God (1 Pet. 1:5).

FAITH CAN BE seen (Matt. 9:2; Mk. 2:5), obeyed (Acts 6:7; Rom. 1:5), turned away (Acts 13:8), and continued in (Acts 14:22; Col. 1:23), be made without effect (Rom. 3:3), be increased (2 Cor. 10:15), examined (2 Cor. 13:5), destroyed (Gal. 1:23), perfected (1 Thess. 3:10), shipwrecked (1 Tim. 1:19) and departed from (1 Tim. 4:1).

FAITH CAN BE denied (1 Tim. 5:8; Rev. 2:13), cast off (1 Tim. 5:12), erred from (1

Tim. 6:10, 21), overthrown (2 Tim. 2:18), followed (2 Tim. 2:22), rejected (2 Tim. 3:8), made sound (Titus 1:13; 2:2), kept (2 Tim. 4: 7), and tried (Jas. 1:3; 1 Pet. 1:7; 5:9).

NOTES